WHO ARE YOU?

JP Publications

Po Box 80581
Seattle, WA 98108

Text and Illustrations
Copyright © 2016

Story by Jennifer Petrone

Illustrations
by
Albert Saavedra

YOU ARE

A GIFT

YOU ARE

PRECIOUS

YOU ARE

BRIGHT
SUNSHINE

YOU ARE

A MIRACLE

YOU ARE

AMAZING

YOU ARE

LOVE

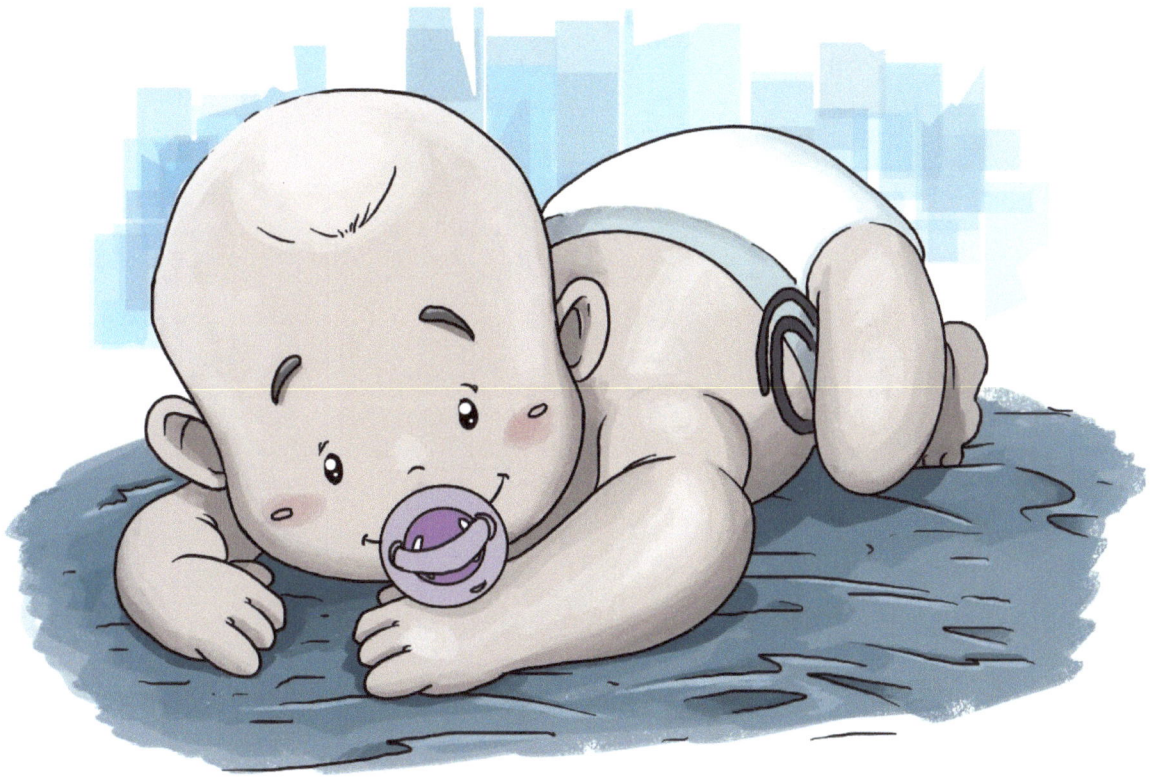

WHERE DID YOU

COME FROM

YOU CAME FROM

HEAVEN

YOU CAME FROM

LOVE

WHAT WILL YOU BECOME?

WILL YOU BE A

DOCTOR
AND HEAL THE WORLD?

WILL YOU BE A

ARCHITECT
AND BUILD BEAUTIFUL
BUILDINGS?

WILL YOU BE A

CHEF
AND FEED THE
HUNGRY?

OR A

SCIENTIST
TO DISCOVER THE SECRETS
OF THE UNIVERSE?

OR MAYBE

EVEN A
VETERINARIAN
TO HELP THE ANIMALS

YOU CAN BE

ANYTHING
YOU WANT TO BE

YOU WILL BE...

WHAT YOU BELIEVE
YOU CAN BE

SO...

BE

WHO YOU
ARE

CELEBRATE

WHO YOU
ARE

EMBRACE

WHO YOU
ARE

YOU ARE
LIFE

AND...

I LOVE YOU

www.ingramcontent.com/pod-product-compliance
Lightning Source LLC
Chambersburg PA
CBHW042118040426
42449CB00002B/85